ONLINE

Make Money Worldwide

TOP 20 WAYS

CONTETNT

Copyright Notice & Disclaimer
Introduction

Simple Online Jobs	1
Through Blogging	2
Freelance Gigs	3
Through Vlogging	4
Sell Photos Online	5
Affiliate Marketing	6
Social Media Marketing	7
Online Consultancy	8
SEO Services	9
Manager of Social Media	10
Developing Mobile Apps	11
Tutoring Online	12
Podcasting	13
Creating & Selling E-Books	14
Selling courses Online	15
Write articles for other	16
Become a Youtuber	17
Sell your notes	18
Sell logo and design work	19
Start a digital marketing	20

Copyright Notice & Disclaimer

©Profit Passive Streams 2021

The authors do not guarantee the results or financial returns you will receive based on this information. It is only for illustrative and educational purposes if specific concepts, techniques, tactics, or ideas are mentioned.

You decide to properly plan, resource, record, and execute what we share (or not). After all, we can lead a horse to water but not make it drink.

Although we have made every attempt to present the most up-to-date knowledge and innovative ideas at the time of writing, we cannot guarantee your future profitability and make no guarantees, either verbally or in writing, that you will earn improved profits if you employ what we share.

At the end of the day, you are the one who makes all the decisions. No guarantee using the information offered will result in success.

Different outcomes may be experienced by a business owner dependent on a variety of external factors that the authors have no control over or influence over.

INTRODUCTION
Profit Passive Streams
Top 20 Ways to Make Money (Easy & Without/low Investment)

Do you know that there could be a hundred different ways to make money online? Anyone with a computer or mobile phone with an Internet connection can do it worldwide.

I've been making money online since 2015, and after years of research and experience, I decided to create a list of the best Top 20 ways to make money online in this book. Whatever your skillset or level of experience, the internet offers a lot of ways to make money. In most circumstances, it's also quick and easy to get started, with no equipment or initial investment required. Because you can use the internet from anywhere in the world, you may pick and choose which of these ideas to use as and when you need to make money.

So, let's have a look at this list of Top 20 best ways that will assist you in making money online.

1. SIMPLE ONLINE JOBS TO MAKE MONEY

This is the first job I suggest to anyone interested in making money online. Micro jobs entail performing small tasks such as reading emails, filling out surveys, viewing movies, and leaving comments.

You can find some most popular sites on Google that will pay you to do tasks.

Pros:
1. Best Money-Making Side Hustle
2. No Skills Necessary
3. No Qualifications Necessary
4. Excellent Stress Relievers
5. Time Pass

Cons:
1. Area-Specific Online Surveys
2. Pay less.
3. There will be no daily surveys.
4. Suspension or cancellation of an account

2. EARN MONEY THROUGH BLOGGING

If you want to make a lot of money, say more than $1000 per month, blogging is the only straightforward and safe way to do so.

While it may take some time at first, once you become an expert, there is nothing like blogging to give you both time freedom and a massive income.

Pros:

1. It's simple to start a blog.
2. It's a less-cost investment.
3. You establish yourself as an authority figure.
4. You can earn money in various ways.
5. Build strong bonds with your audience.

Cons:

1. It takes a long time.
2. Problems with the technology
3. Making money takes time.
4. An excellent blog should be updated on a regular basis.

3. FREELANCE GIGS

Freelancing is the third most popular way for people to make a lot of money on the internet.

There are large numbers of popular freelance sites where you can find hundreds of different jobs to do for your clients. You can offer writing, web design, data entry, virtual assistant, SEO, video maker, video editing, graphic design, and many other services.

Pros:
1. Work Schedule Flexibility
2. Control on Jobs and Clients
3. Work From Anywhere You Want
4. You're the Boss
5. Keep all the Profits

Cons:
1. Cash Flow Issues
2. Ultimate Responsibility
3. Sporadic Work
4. Sometimes Late Payments

4. EARN MONEY THROUGH VLOGGING

Vlogging or video blogging, is the process of creating and uploading great videos to YouTube or other video sharing sites. If your videos are unique and popular, you can earn money by partnering with Google. Thousands of people make a good living by running their own YouTube channel.

Pros:
1. Ton of Fun
2. The Moments will be Saved
3. Making Vlogs is completely free
4. More Content ideas

Cons:
1. Expensive in terms of time
2. Lack of privacy
3. Need 100% commitment

5. SELL PHOTOS ONLINE

Are you a keen photographer? Selling stock photos is an excellent way to monetize your hobby. Companies will typically buy a subscription to a stock agency, which grants them the right to use any stock image on the site for the duration of their subscription.

Selling stock photos is a great way to earn a side income, but it's difficult to turn into a full-time job.

Pros:
1. A large client base
2. Worldwide reach
3. Self-employment
4. Passive income

Cons:
1. Low price
2. Rejection rate is high.
3. Income growth is slow in the beginning

6. AFFILIATE MARKETING

Affiliate marketing is the process of making money (commissions) for promoting a company's products or services and resulting in a sale. You are only paid when you drive a sale, just like a commission-only sales representative. Affiliate marketing can be described as a process of spreading product development and marketing across multiple parties, with each party receiving a percentage of the revenue based on their contribution.

Pros:
1. Zero/low investment
2. Passive Income
3. Billion-Dollar Business
4. Beginner Friendly
5. High Income Potential

Cons:
1. Commission-Based Payout
2. Requires a great deal of patience and hard work
3. High Competition

7. SOCIAL MEDIA MARKETING

Social media marketing, is a type of internet marketing that involves creating and sharing content on social media networks in order to achieve marketing and branding objectives. Social media marketing covers areas such as posting text and image updates, videos, and other content that encourages audience engagement, as well as paid social media advertising.

Pros:
1. low investment
2. Passive Income
3. Billion-Dollar Business
4. Beginner Friendly
5. High Income Potential

Cons:
1. Commission-Based Payout
2. Requires a great deal of patience and hard work
3. High Competition

8. ONLINE CONSULTANCY

This is best suited for people who have expertise in a specific field. You can start an online consultancy if you are a teacher, doctor, trainer, or anyone else who has skills that can help others solve their problems.

You can advertise your services on your blog, Google+, Facebook, and other social media platforms. You can provide consultation over the phone or via Skype.

Pros:

1. You are not required to be a personal expert.
2. You are NOT a worker bee.
3. You can generate income from the success of others.
4. You need a low-cost setup.
5. High Income Potential

Cons:

1. Practical experience needed
2. Lot of competition
3. Less control over the outcome

9. SEO SERVICES

SEO, or search engine optimization, is very popular. A number of businesses are looking for an SEO expert to help them rank their website high on Google.

Go for it if you have experience and know everything there is to know about SEO. You can either start your own SEO company or work as a freelancer.

Pros:

1. Results are not instantaneous
2. Contract choice.
3. You have control
4. You need a low-cost setup.
5. High Income Potential

Cons:

1. Difficult to Achieve
2. Lot of competition
3. Volatility

10. EXECUTIVE / MANAGER OF SOCIAL MEDIA

Similarly, businesses require a social media manager to manage their operations on Facebook, Twitter, and YouTube, along with many other platforms.

You must have prior experience with social media platforms. There is also the possibility of managing the Twitter accounts of celebrities, businesses, or other significant individuals, where you will tweet on their behalf and manage their followers and responses.

Pros:
1. Opportunities are endless
2. Contract choice.
3. You can learn a lot
4. it's fast interaction
5. High Income Potential

Cons:
1. You have to deal with complaints
2. It can be very stressful.

11. DEVELOPING MOBILE APPS

App development for Android or iOS devices has always been a profitable venture. You can make a lot of money if you can create an innovative app that solves people's problems.

However, you must have prior coding experience. You can also get work from businesses and individuals to create a customized application for their products or services.

Pros:
1. Opportunities are endless
2. Contract choice.
3. You can learn a lot
4. High Income Potential
5. Promotional Opportunities

Cons:
1. Time-consuming
2. It can be very stressful.
3. Competition is high

12. TUTORING ONLINE

Tutoring jobs can be found on websites such as Tutor.com. You will be teaching children online using Skype or other software. You can select a subject that you are most knowledgeable about.

Pros:
1. Opportunities are endless
2. Choice in Subject.
3. You can learn a lot
4. More Comfortable
5. Low Investment

Cons:
1. It is more difficult to establish a relationship with a student.
2. Technology-related problems.
3. Competition is high

13. PODCASTING

Podcasting is an excellent way to earn money online. If you are knowledgeable about a subject, such as finance or current events, you can record videos and sell them online. People are willing to pay a few dollars for your podcast videos.

Pros:
1. Opportunities are endless
2. Convenience
3. You can learn a lot
4. No restriction on time
5. Not a very expensive

Cons:
1. Content protection is difficult.
2. Technology-related problems.
3. Takes a lot of time

14. CREATING & SELLING E-BOOKS

Create eBooks and sell them online. If you are knowledgeable about a particular subject, such as dog training, cooking, music, or marketing, you can create an eBook and sell it online for $1 or $20 per copy, depending on your own valuation.

Pros:
1. No trees die
2. eBooks are portable
3. You can learn a lot
4. Instant download
5. More Passive Income

Cons:
1. Ebooks have a lower perceived value.
2. Ebook creation has a learning curve.
3. Takes a lot of time.

15. SELLING COURSES ONLINE

You can create courses in the form of eBooks or Podcasts and sell them online. You can become a vendor on Clickbank and utilize the services of other affiliate marketers.

These courses could be about cooking, how to start a blog, photography, and so on.

Pros:
1. Opportunities are endless
2. Choice in Subject.
3. You can learn a lot
4. More Comfortable
5. Low Investment

Cons:
1. It is more difficult to establish a relationship with a student.
2. Technology-related problems.
3. Competition is high

16. WRITE ARTICLES FOR OTHER SITES

If you are unable to start your own blog, you can write for other well-known websites or bloggers on the internet.

You can meet with them in person to discuss rates for each blog post you write.

If you want to make a lot of money from this, your writing skills must be exceptional. There are websites that will pay you up to $200 per post.

Pros:
1. Opportunities are endless
2. Choice in Subject.
3. You can learn and earn a lot
4. Easy Work.
5. Low Investment

Cons:
1. Low price
2. Rejection rate is high.
3. Income growth is slow at the beginning
4. Competition is high

17. BECOME A YOUTUBER

It takes a lot of effort to become a successful YouTuber. You'll need to be consistent with your uploads and pick a popular niche, such as daily vlogs, gaming, or tech videos. Every month, YouTube pays YouTubers 45 to 50 percent of ad revenue. These figures equate to an average of £5 to £7 per 1000 views, indicating that you can generate a large passive income from old videos. You can also do paid promotions.

Pros:
1. Opportunities are endless
2. YouTube channels can make you famous
3. You can learn and earn a lot
4. Low Investment

Cons:
1. Time Consuming
2. YouTube can be a very competitive environment.
3. Editing can be irritating.
4. Income growth is slow at the beginning
5. People may steal your ideas

18. SELL YOUR NOTES

Are you a student looking for a quick way to make money? If you answered yes, selling your study materials online through sites like Stuvia and studypool is a great way to make money. Stuvia is used by over 175,000 students to collect notes for subjects such as law, chemistry, and medicine, to name a few.

Pros:
1. Opportunities are endless
2. Helping Other
3. You can learn and earn a lot
4. Zero Investment

Cons:
1. Time Consuming
2. Low price
4. Income growth is slow at the beginning
5. People may steal your ideas

19. SELL LOGO AND DESIGN WORK

Logos are essential to a company's brand identity, so you can charge a lot of money for them. Every year, approximately 660,000 new businesses are established in the United Kingdom, resulting in high demand for new logos and design work.

Pros:
1. Steadydemand for designer
2. More Money
3. You can learn and earn a lot
4. Zero Investment

Cons:
1. Time Consuming
2. Not easy
3. Very high competition
4. People may steal your ideas

20. Start a digital marketing

You will provide business services such as SEO (search engine optimization), SMM (social media marketing), paid marketing, copywriting, and content writing as a digital marketer. Your responsibilities will range from consulting on marketing strategy to full management of a company's ad campaign. When it comes to growing a business, businesses understand that marketing is everything. To launch a digital marketing agency, you must have prior experience in advertising or marketing via digital media.

Pros:
1. Steady demand for Digital Marketers
2. Digital marketers can earn good money.
3. You can learn and earn a lot.
4. Digital marketers can work from home.
5. Help companies to scale their business

Cons:
1. Being a digital marketer can be challenging.
2. Not easy
3. Very high competition
4. Online marketing is a long-term effort.

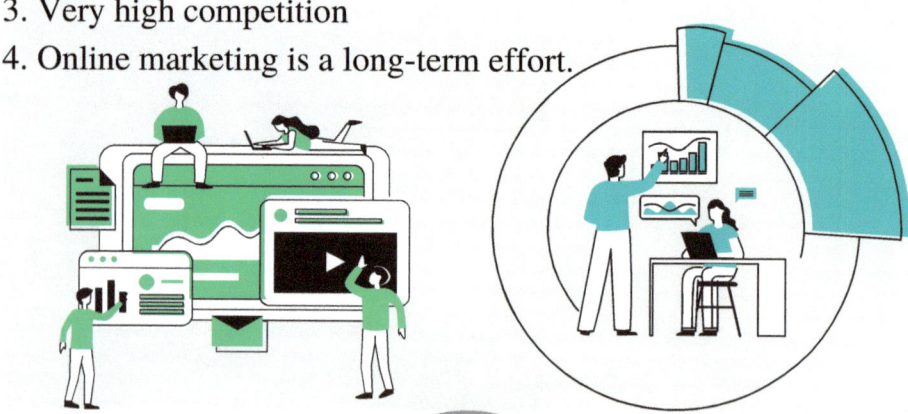

Thank You

www.ingramcontent.com/pod-product-compliance
Lightning Source LLC
Chambersburg PA
CBHW040351220526
45473CB00009B/2851